TO:

FROM:

Blessed

LIVE, TRAVEL, ADVENTURE, BLESS, AND DON'T BE SORRY.

JACK KEROUAC

Blessed

WRITTEN AND
COMPILED BY
ELIZABETH LEGAN

PETER PAUPER PRESS, INC.
White Plains, New York

For Bruce and Karen Legan.
I'm blessed to have you in my corner.

Designed by Margaret Rubiano

Copyright © 2016
Peter Pauper Press, Inc.
202 Mamaroneck Avenue
White Plains, NY 10601
All rights reserved
ISBN 978-1-4413-2126-8
Printed in China
7 6 5 4 3 2

Visit us at www.peterpauper.com

Blessed is about being grateful. Blessed is a state of mind, an attitude. Blessed is all about your perception of your world. What if you reserved a moment each day to pause and reflect on all the good around you? While that pause might be shorter on some days than on others, simply pausing allows you to focus on the important things in life: being grateful, giving to others, and seizing the day.

Blessed

ARE THEY WHO SEE
BEAUTIFUL THINGS IN
HUMBLE PLACES WHERE
OTHER PEOPLE
SEE NOTHING.

CAMILLE PISSARRO

LET US BE

grateful

TO PEOPLE WHO MAKE US
HAPPY; THEY ARE THE
CHARMING GARDENERS
WHO MAKE OUR
SOULS BLOSSOM.

MARCEL PROUST

The world only exists

IN YOUR EYES.
YOU CAN MAKE IT
AS BIG OR AS SMALL
AS YOU WANT.

F. SCOTT FITZGERALD

The more grateful we are,

THE MORE WE PRACTICE
THIS IN OUR EVERYDAY
LIVES, THE MORE CONNECTED
WE BECOME TO THE
UNIVERSE AROUND US.

STEPHEN RICHARDS

Today is gone.
Today was fun.
Tomorrow is
another one.

DR. SEUSS

GRATITUDE UNLOCKS THE
FULLNESS OF LIFE.
IT TURNS WHAT WE HAVE
INTO ENOUGH, AND MORE.
IT TURNS DENIAL INTO
ACCEPTANCE, CHAOS TO ORDER,
CONFUSION TO CLARITY. IT CAN
TURN A MEAL INTO A FEAST, A
HOUSE INTO A HOME, A
STRANGER INTO A FRIEND.

MELODY BEATTIE

Reflect upon your
present blessings—
OF WHICH EVERY MAN HAS
MANY—NOT ON YOUR PAST
MISFORTUNES, OF WHICH ALL
MEN HAVE SOME.

CHARLES DICKENS

EXPECT TO HAVE
hope rekindled.
EXPECT YOUR PRAYERS TO
BE ANSWERED IN WONDROUS
WAYS. THE DRY SEASONS IN LIFE
DO NOT LAST. THE SPRING
RAINS WILL COME AGAIN.

SARAH BAN BREATHNACH

THE PERSON WHO
CAN BRING THE SPIRIT
OF LAUGHTER INTO
A ROOM IS
INDEED BLESSED.

BENNETT CERF

Be grateful for
whoever comes,
because each has
been sent as
a guide from
beyond.

RUMI

EACH DAY OFFERS US
THE GIFT OF BEING A SPECIAL
OCCASION IF WE CAN SIMPLY
LEARN THAT AS WELL AS GIVING,

*it is blessed
to receive*

WITH GRACE AND
A GRATEFUL HEART.

SARAH BAN BREATHNACH

"DEAR OLD WORLD,"
SHE MURMURED,
"YOU ARE VERY LOVELY,
AND I AM GLAD TO BE
alive in you."

L.M. MONTGOMERY

I AM ETERNALLY
GRATEFUL FOR MY
KNACK OF FINDING IN
GREAT BOOKS, SOME OF
THEM VERY FUNNY BOOKS,
REASON ENOUGH TO FEEL
HONORED TO BE ALIVE,
NO MATTER WHAT ELSE
MIGHT BE GOING ON.

KURT VONNEGUT

She taught
me to respect
the hand that
I was dealt.
And to be
grateful I was
even dealt
a hand.

COLLEEN HOOVER

THIS IS THE KEY TO LIFE:
TO EXPECT EVERYTHING TO BE
GIVEN TO YOU FROM ABOVE, YET TO
BE GENUINELY SURPRISED AND FOREVER
GRATEFUL WHEN THEY ARE. EXPECTING
ALL GOOD THINGS TO BE YOURS, WHILE
NOT KNOWING HOW TO TAKE ANYTHING
FOR GRANTED. IF THERE MAY BE A
KEY IN LIFE, THIS IS THE KEY.

C. JOYBELL C.

I BELIEVE THE
ABILITY TO THINK IS
blessed.
IF YOU CAN THINK ABOUT
A SITUATION, YOU CAN DEAL
WITH IT. THE BIG STRUGGLE IS
TO KEEP YOUR HEAD CLEAR
ENOUGH TO THINK.

RICHARD PRYOR

Immensely grateful, touched, proud, astonished, abashed.

BORIS PASTERNAK

BUT I HAVE FOUND THAT IN THE
SIMPLE ACT OF LIVING WITH HOPE,
AND IN THE DAILY EFFORT TO HAVE A
POSITIVE IMPACT IN THE WORLD, THE
DAYS I DO HAVE ARE MADE ALL THE
MORE MEANINGFUL AND PRECIOUS.
AND FOR THAT I AM GRATEFUL.

ELIZABETH EDWARDS

I HAVE FOUND
THAT IF YOU
love life,
LIFE WILL
LOVE YOU BACK.

ARTHUR RUBINSTEIN

TODAY, I AM BLESSED
TO BE LIVING A DREAM.
AND YET, IF IT ALL WENT
AWAY TOMORROW, I KNOW
I WOULD STILL HAVE PEACE.

TIM HOWARD

I COUNT AS BLESSINGS
THINGS I COULD HAVE
BENEFITED FROM, EVEN
IF I NEGLECTED TO UTILIZE
THEM. A GIFT IS STILL A GIFT,
EVEN IF LEFT WRAPPED
AND UNOPENED.

JAROD KINTZ

Be grateful

FOR WHAT YOU HAVE AND
STOP COMPLAINING—IT BORES
EVERYBODY ELSE, DOES YOU
NO GOOD, AND DOESN'T
SOLVE ANY PROBLEMS.

ZIG ZIGLAR

LEARN TO GET IN TOUCH WITH
THE SILENCE WITHIN YOURSELF
AND KNOW THAT EVERYTHING IN
LIFE HAS PURPOSE, THERE ARE NO
MISTAKES, NO COINCIDENCES,
ALL EVENTS ARE BLESSINGS
GIVEN TO US TO LEARN FROM.

ELISABETH KÜBLER-ROSS

When we give
cheerfully and
accept gratefully,
everyone
is blessed.

MAYA ANGELOU

I WAKE UP AND REALIZE
THAT WHAT SEEMED TO
BE IMPORTANT LAST YEAR
NO LONGER IS. I'M
INCREASINGLY GRATEFUL
FOR EVERY DAY.

VAL KILMER

Each day holds a surprise.

BUT ONLY IF WE EXPECT IT CAN WE SEE, HEAR, OR FEEL IT WHEN IT COMES TO US. LET'S NOT BE AFRAID TO RECEIVE EACH DAY'S SURPRISE, WHETHER IT COMES TO US AS SORROW OR AS JOY.

HENRI J.M. NOUWEN

Be thankful for what you have; YOU'LL END UP HAVING MORE. IF YOU CONCENTRATE ON WHAT YOU DON'T HAVE, YOU WILL NEVER, EVER HAVE ENOUGH.

OPRAH WINFREY

EVERYTHING HAS
ITS WONDERS, EVEN
DARKNESS AND SILENCE,
AND I LEARN, WHATEVER
STATE I MAY BE IN,
THEREIN TO BE CONTENT.

HELEN KELLER

True happiness is
to enjoy the present,
WITHOUT ANXIOUS DEPENDENCE
UPON THE FUTURE, NOT TO
AMUSE OURSELVES WITH EITHER
HOPES OR FEARS BUT TO REST
SATISFIED WITH WHAT WE
HAVE, WHICH IS SUFFICIENT,

FOR HE THAT IS SO
WANTS NOTHING. THE GREAT
BLESSINGS OF MANKIND ARE
WITHIN US AND WITHIN OUR REACH.
A WISE MAN IS CONTENT WITH
HIS LOT, WHATEVER IT MAY
BE, WITHOUT WISHING
FOR WHAT HE HAS NOT.

SENECA THE YOUNGER

GRATITUDE IS A MARK
OF A NOBLE SOUL AND A
REFINED CHARACTER. WE LIKE
TO BE AROUND THOSE WHO
ARE GRATEFUL.

JOSEPH B. WIRTHLIN

I'm so glad
I live in a world
where there are
Octobers.

L.M. MONTGOMERY

MAKE IT A HABIT TO TELL PEOPLE "THANK YOU." TO EXPRESS YOUR APPRECIATION, SINCERELY AND WITHOUT THE EXPECTATION OF ANYTHING IN RETURN. TRULY APPRECIATE THOSE AROUND YOU, AND YOU'LL SOON FIND MANY OTHERS AROUND YOU. TRULY APPRECIATE LIFE, AND YOU'LL FIND THAT YOU HAVE MORE OF IT.

RALPH MARSTON

The madness of love

IS THE GREATEST OF HEAVEN'S BLESSINGS.

PLATO

BE GRATEFUL FOR LUCK.
PAY THE THUNDER NO
MIND—LISTEN TO THE
BIRDS. AND DON'T
HATE NOBODY.

EUBIE BLAKE

Never to suffer would have been never to have been blessed.

EDGAR ALLAN POE

But listen to me:
for one moment,
quit being sad. Hear
blessings dropping
their blossoms
around you.

RUMI

IT IS NECESSARY, THEN,
TO CULTIVATE THE HABIT OF BEING
GRATEFUL FOR EVERY GOOD THING THAT
COMES TO YOU; AND TO GIVE THANKS
CONTINUOUSLY. AND BECAUSE ALL THINGS
HAVE CONTRIBUTED TO YOUR
ADVANCEMENT, YOU SHOULD INCLUDE
ALL THINGS IN YOUR GRATITUDE.

WALLACE D. WATTLES

I'M A GREAT
BELIEVER IN LUCK.
The harder I work,
THE MORE OF IT
I SEEM TO HAVE.

COLEMAN COX

BE CONTENT WITH
WHAT YOU HAVE; REJOICE
IN THE WAY THINGS ARE.
WHEN YOU REALIZE THERE
IS NOTHING LACKING,
THE WHOLE WORLD
BELONGS TO YOU.

LAO TZU

I THANK YOU GOD FOR MOST
THIS AMAZING DAY: FOR THE
LEAPING GREENLY SPIRITS OF TREES
AND A BLUE TRUE DREAM OF SKY;
AND FOR EVERYTHING WHICH
IS NATURAL, WHICH IS INFINITE,
WHICH IS YES.

E.E. CUMMINGS

Be present in all things and thankful for all things.

MAYA ANGELOU

Live your truth.
EXPRESS YOUR LOVE. SHARE YOUR
ENTHUSIASM. TAKE ACTION TOWARDS
YOUR DREAMS. WALK YOUR TALK.
DANCE AND SING TO YOUR MUSIC.
EMBRACE YOUR BLESSINGS. MAKE
TODAY WORTH REMEMBERING.

STEVE MARABOLI

YOUR DREAMS,
WHAT YOU HOPE FOR
AND ALL THAT, IT'S NOT
SEPARATE FROM YOUR LIFE.
*It grows right
up out of it.*

BARBARA KINGSOLVER

When you
are grateful—
WHEN YOU CAN SEE WHAT YOU
HAVE—YOU UNLOCK BLESSINGS
TO FLOW IN YOUR LIFE.

SUZE ORMAN

BUT WHY THINK ABOUT
THAT WHEN ALL THE GOLDEN
LAND'S AHEAD OF YOU AND
ALL KINDS OF UNFORESEEN
EVENTS WAIT LURKING TO
SURPRISE YOU AND
MAKE YOU GLAD YOU'RE
ALIVE TO SEE?

JACK KEROUAC

IF THE ONLY PRAYER
YOU EVER SAY IN YOUR
ENTIRE LIFE IS THANK YOU,
IT WILL BE ENOUGH.

MEISTER ECKHART

If you want to be happy, be.

ALEKSEY KONSTANTINOVICH TOLSTOY

As the years pass,
I AM COMING MORE AND MORE
TO UNDERSTAND THAT IT IS THE
COMMON, EVERYDAY BLESSINGS
OF OUR COMMON EVERYDAY LIVES
FOR WHICH WE SHOULD BE
PARTICULARLY GRATEFUL. THEY ARE
THE THINGS THAT FILL OUR LIVES
WITH COMFORT AND OUR HEARTS

WITH GLADNESS—JUST THE PURE AIR
TO BREATHE AND THE STRENGTH
TO BREATHE IT; JUST WARMTH
AND SHELTER AND HOME FOLKS;
JUST PLAIN FOOD THAT GIVES US
STRENGTH; THE BRIGHT SUNSHINE
ON A COLD DAY; AND A COOL
BREEZE WHEN THE DAY IS WARM.

LAURA INGALLS WILDER

FREE YOURSELF FROM THE COMPLEXITIES
AND DRAMA OF YOUR LIFE.

Simplify.

LOOK WITHIN. WITHIN OURSELVES
WE ALL HAVE THE GIFTS AND TALENTS
WE NEED TO FULFILL THE PURPOSE
WE'VE BEEN BLESSED WITH.

STEVE MARABOLI

Most of the time, all you have is the moment, and the imperfect love of the people around you.

ANNE LAMOTT

I'M JUST THANKFUL FOR EVERYTHING, ALL THE BLESSINGS IN MY LIFE, TRYING TO STAY THAT WAY. I THINK THAT'S THE BEST WAY TO START YOUR DAY AND FINISH YOUR DAY. IT KEEPS EVERYTHING IN PERSPECTIVE.

TIM TEBOW

Because when
you stop and look
around, this life
is pretty amazing.

AUTHOR UNKNOWN

OFTEN, TOO, OUR OWN
LIGHT GOES OUT AND IS

rekindled

BY SOME EXPERIENCE WE GO
THROUGH WITH A FELLOW MAN.
THUS WE HAVE EACH OF US
CAUSE TO THINK WITH DEEP
GRATITUDE OF THOSE WHO HAVE
LIGHTED THE FLAMES WITHIN US.

ALBERT SCHWEITZER

THERE IS NO GREATER
FULFILLMENT AS THE

pursuit of
dreams.

LAILAH GIFTY AKITA

"THANK YOU" IS THE BEST PRAYER THAT ANYONE COULD SAY. I SAY THAT ONE A LOT. THANK YOU EXPRESSES EXTREME GRATITUDE, HUMILITY, UNDERSTANDING.

ALICE WALKER

Blessed are the hearts which can bend; they shall never be broken.

SAINT FRANCIS DE SALES

PURSUE SOME PATH, HOWEVER NARROW AND CROOKED, IN WHICH YOU CAN WALK WITH *love and reverence.*

HENRY DAVID THOREAU

I WORK VERY HARD,
AND I PLAY VERY HARD.
I'm grateful for life.
AND I LIVE IT—
I BELIEVE LIFE LOVES THE
LIVER OF IT. I LIVE IT.

MAYA ANGELOU

YOUR SUCCESS AND
HAPPINESS LIE IN YOU.
RESOLVE TO KEEP HAPPY,
AND YOUR JOY AND
YOU SHALL FORM AN
INVINCIBLE HOST
AGAINST DIFFICULTIES.

HELEN KELLER

WHEN WE LOSE
ONE BLESSING,
ANOTHER IS OFTEN
MOST UNEXPECTEDLY
GIVEN IN ITS PLACE.

C.S. LEWIS

LET'S RISE UP AND BE THANKFUL,
FOR IF WE DIDN'T LEARN A LOT
TODAY, AT LEAST WE LEARNED A
LITTLE. AND IF WE DIDN'T LEARN
A LITTLE, AT LEAST WE DIDN'T
GET SICK. AND IF WE GOT SICK, AT
LEAST WE DIDN'T DIE. SO LET US
ALL BE THANKFUL.

LEO BUSCAGLIA

It is one of the
blessings of old
friends that you
can afford to be
stupid with them.

RALPH WALDO EMERSON

KIND WORDS ARE A CREATIVE
FORCE, A POWER THAT
CONCURS IN THE BUILDING UP
OF ALL THAT IS GOOD, AND
ENERGY THAT SHOWERS
BLESSINGS UPON THE WORLD.

LAWRENCE G. LOVASIK

Trust yourself.
YOU KNOW MORE THAN
YOU THINK YOU DO.

BENJAMIN SPOCK

WHAT IF YOU GAVE SOMEONE
A GIFT, AND THEY NEGLECTED TO
THANK YOU FOR IT—WOULD YOU
BE LIKELY TO GIVE THEM ANOTHER?
LIFE IS THE SAME WAY. IN ORDER
TO ATTRACT MORE OF THE
BLESSINGS THAT LIFE HAS TO
OFFER, YOU MUST TRULY
APPRECIATE WHAT YOU
ALREADY HAVE.

RALPH MARSTON

A true friend

IS THE GREATEST OF ALL BLESSINGS.

FRANCOIS DE LA ROCHEFOUCAULD

Gratitude

CAN TRANSFORM COMMON
DAYS INTO THANKSGIVINGS,
TURN ROUTINE JOBS INTO JOY,
AND CHANGE ORDINARY
OPPORTUNITIES INTO BLESSINGS.

WILLIAM ARTHUR WARD

LET ME ENCOURAGE YOU
TO GET UP EVERY DAY AND FOCUS
ON WHAT YOU DO HAVE IN LIFE.

Be thankful

FOR THE BLESSINGS OF THE LITTLE
THINGS, EVEN WHEN YOU DON'T GET
WHAT YOU EXPECT.

VICTORIA OSTEEN

TURN YOUR

attention

FOR A WHILE AWAY FROM
THE WORRIES AND ANXIETIES.
REMIND YOURSELF OF ALL
YOUR MANY BLESSINGS.

RALPH MARSTON

THE MOST
beautiful people
WE HAVE KNOWN ARE THOSE
WHO HAVE KNOWN DEFEAT,
KNOWN SUFFERING, KNOWN
STRUGGLE, KNOWN LOSS, AND
HAVE FOUND THEIR WAY OUT
OF THOSE DEPTHS.

ELISABETH KÜBLER-ROSS

When I started counting my blessings, my whole life turned around.

WILLIE NELSON

THE MOMENTS OF
HAPPINESS WE ENJOY TAKE
US BY SURPRISE. IT IS NOT
THAT WE SEIZE THEM, BUT
THAT THEY SEIZE US.

ASHLEY MONTAGU

TRY TO MAKE AT LEAST ONE PERSON
happy every day.
IF YOU CANNOT DO A KIND DEED,
SPEAK A KIND WORD. IF YOU CANNOT
SPEAK A KIND WORD, THINK A KIND
THOUGHT. COUNT UP, IF YOU CAN,
THE TREASURE OF HAPPINESS THAT
YOU WOULD DISPENSE IN A WEEK,
IN A YEAR, IN A LIFETIME!

LAWRENCE G. LOVASIK

OF THE BLESSINGS SET BEFORE YOU MAKE YOUR CHOICE, AND *be content.*

SAMUEL JOHNSON

We love and we lose,
GO BACK TO THE START AND DO IT RIGHT
OVER AGAIN. FOR EVERY HEAVY FOREBRAIN
SOLEMNLY CATALOGING THE FACTS OF A HARSH
LANDSCAPE, THERE'S A RUSH OF INTUITION
BEHIND IT CRYING OUT: HIGH TIDE! TIME TO
MOVE OUT INTO THE GLORIOUS DEBRIS.
TIME TO TAKE THIS LIFE FOR WHAT IT IS.

BARBARA KINGSOLVER

Be happy

WITH WHAT YOU HAVE
AND ARE, BE GENEROUS WITH
BOTH, AND YOU WON'T HAVE
TO HUNT FOR HAPPINESS.

WILLIAM E. GLADSTONE

A hug is like a boomerang—
you get it back right away.

BIL KEANE

I PROFOUNDLY FEEL THAT
THE ART OF LIVING IS THE ART OF
GIVING. YOU'RE FULFILLED IN THE
MOMENT OF GIVING, OF DOING
SOMETHING BEYOND YOURSELF.

LAURANCE ROCKEFELLER

THE MORE YOU FIND
OUT ABOUT THE WORLD,
THE MORE OPPORTUNITIES
THERE ARE TO
laugh at it.

BILL NYE

OCCASIONALLY IN LIFE
THERE ARE THOSE MOMENTS
OF UNUTTERABLE FULFILLMENT
WHICH CANNOT BE COMPLETELY
EXPLAINED BY THOSE SYMBOLS
CALLED WORDS. THEIR MEANING
CAN ONLY BE ARTICULATED BY THE
INAUDIBLE LANGUAGE OF THE HEART.

MARTIN LUTHER KING, JR.

REMEMBER THAT
SOMETIMES NOT
GETTING WHAT YOU
WANT IS A WONDERFUL
STROKE OF LUCK.

JACKSON BROWN AND H. JACKSON BROWN, JR.

THERE ARE

better things

AHEAD THAN ANY
WE LEAVE BEHIND.

C.S. LEWIS

THERE WERE ABOUT
SEVENTY-NINE SQUILLION
PEOPLE IN THE WORLD, AND
IF YOU WERE VERY LUCKY,
YOU WOULD END UP BEING
LOVED BY FIFTEEN
OR TWENTY OF THEM.

NICK HORNBY

Blessed are those who give without remembering and take without forgetting.

ELIZABETH BIBESCO

THE THING ABOUT LIGHT
IS THAT IT REALLY ISN'T YOURS;
IT'S WHAT YOU GATHER AND SHINE
BACK. AND IT GETS MORE POWER
FROM REFLECTIVENESS; IF YOU SIT
STILL AND TAKE IT IN, IT FILLS
YOUR CUP, AND THEN YOU CAN
GIVE IT OFF YOURSELF.

ANNE LAMOTT

Thanks for this day,

FOR ALL BIRDS SAFE ·
IN THEIR NESTS, FOR
WHATEVER THIS IS,
FOR LIFE.

BARBARA KINGSOLVER

WITHIN YOU IS A LIMITLESS,
UNBORN POTENTIAL OF
CREATIVITY AND SUBSTANCE,
AND THE PRESENT EXPERIENCE
CAN BE YOUR GREAT
OPPORTUNITY TO GIVE BIRTH TO IT.

ERIC BUTTERWORTH

The dedicated life is the life worth living. You must give with your whole heart.

ANNIE DILLARD

YOU HAVE TO PARTICIPATE RELENTLESSLY IN THE MANIFESTATION OF YOUR OWN BLESSINGS.

ELIZABETH GILBERT

IMAGES USED UNDER LICENSE FROM SHUTTERSTOCK.COM, AS FOLLOWS:

Cover, endpapers, pages 1, 6-7, 20-21, 48-49, 62-63, 76-77, 90-91 © Julianka

Pages 4-5, 8-9, 22-23, 36-37, 50-51, 64-65, 78-79, 92-93 © melazerg

Pages 10-11, 24-25, 38-39, 52-53, 66-67, 80-81, 94-95 © Irbena

Pages 12-13, 26-27, 40-41, 54-55, 68-69, 82-83, 96-back endsheet © xenia_ok

Pages 14-15, 28-29, 42-43, 56-57, 70-71, 84-85 © Ihnatovich Maryia

Pages 2-5, 16-17, 30-31, 34-35, 44-45, 58-59, 72-73, 86-87 © Transia Design

Pages 18-19, 32-33, 46-47, 60-61, 74-75, 88-89 © Mary1507